UPDOG

EXTREME ENDURANCE CHALLENGES

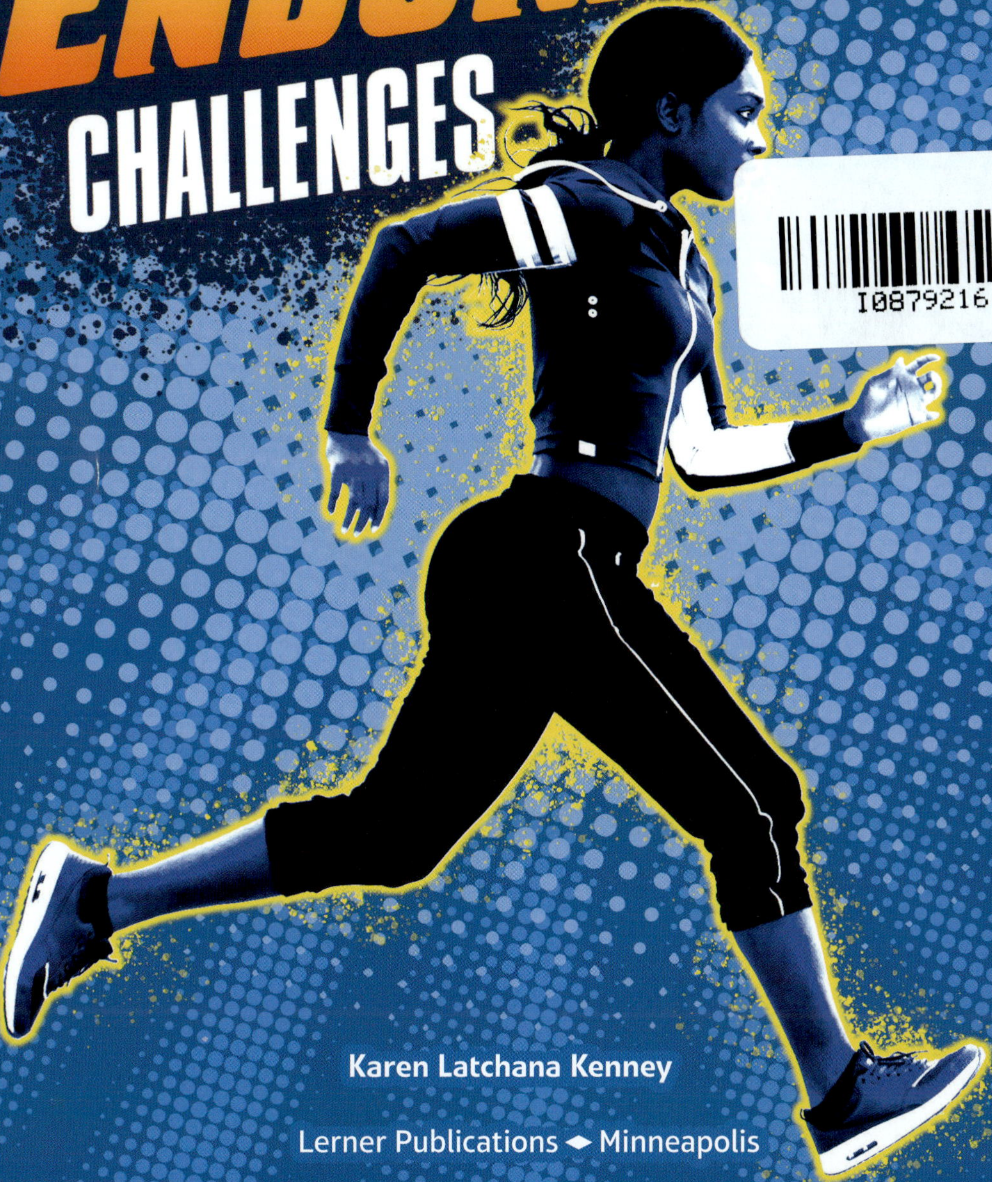

Karen Latchana Kenney

Lerner Publications ◆ Minneapolis

Lerner Publications Company
An imprint of Lerner Publishing Group, Inc.
241 First Avenue North
Minneapolis, MN 55401 USA

For reading levels and more information, look up this title at www.lernerbooks.com.

Main body text set in ITC Franklin Gothic Std.
Typeface provided by Adobe Systems.

Editor: Shee Yang **Designer:** Viet Chu

Library of Congress Cataloging-in-Publication Data

The Cataloging-in-Publication Data for *Extreme Endurance Challenges* is on file at the Library of Congress.

ISBN 978-1-5415-9043-4 (lib. bdg.)
ISBN 978-1-72841-812-4 (eb pdf)

Manufactured in the United States of America
1-47562-48092-5/6/2020

Table of Contents

An Extreme Racer

Eric Hutterer did something few people can do. He finished the Spartan Death Race.

The race lasted 60 hours.
Of the 80 who entered, Hutterer was one of just 12 people to finish.

Endurance challenges are extreme. Racers train hard for them.

endurance: the ability to stay strong over a long period of time

Endurance Hacks

- Drink lots of water. Water will boost your energy.
- Strengthen your legs. You'll need strong legs to keep up.
- Stretch often. Tight muscles will cause injury in an endurance challenge.
- Think positively. A positive attitude goes a long way!

UP NEXT!

Training to finish strong.

Endurance Training

An endurance race takes full body strength. Racers have to train every muscle.

They cross-train. They run, swim, and lift weights.

cross-train: to do two or more workouts that train the whole body

Some competitions last for days. Racers get very little sleep.

They try to stay awake for as long as they can as part of their training.

Bio Break!

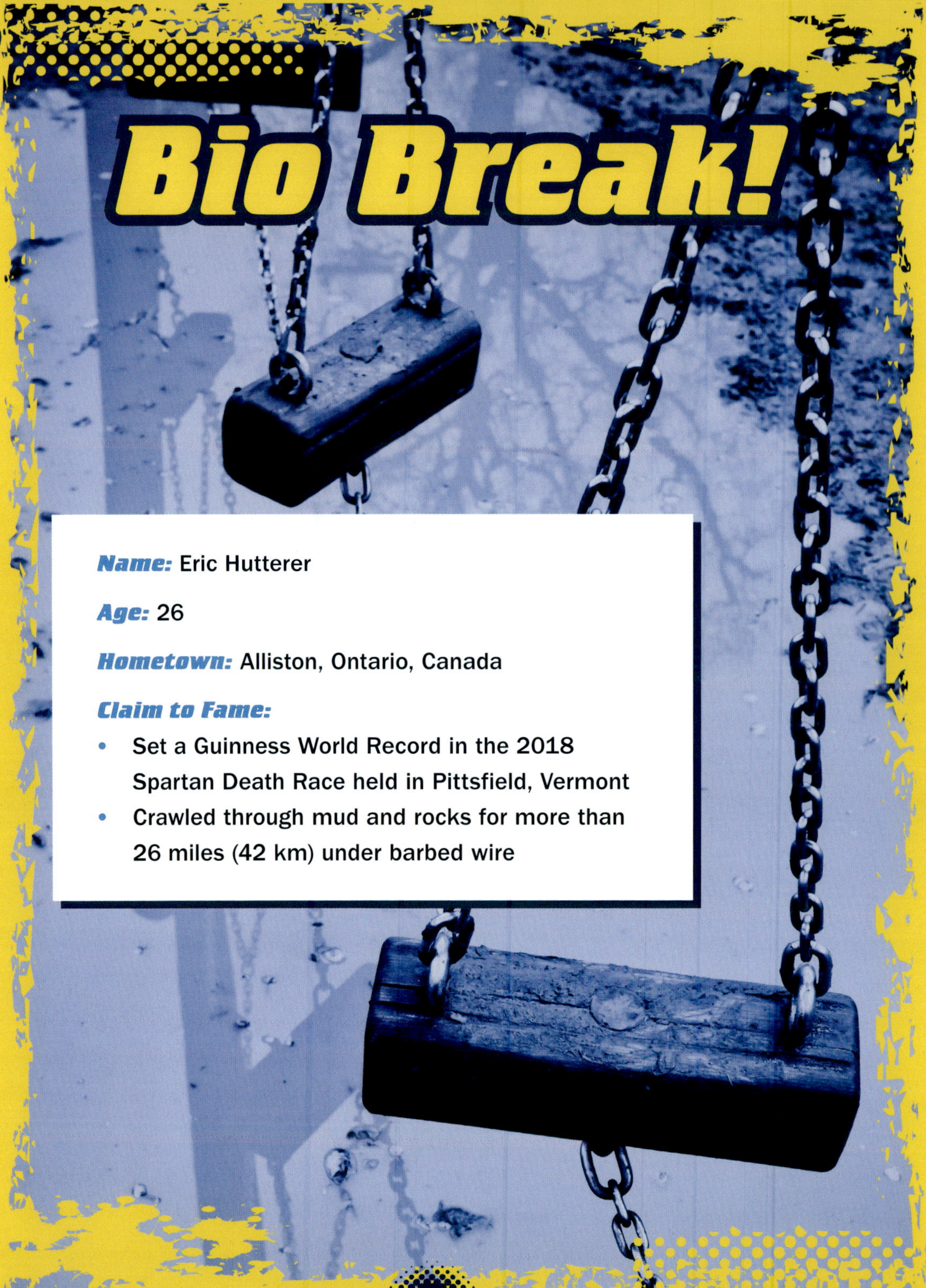

Name: Eric Hutterer

Age: 26

Hometown: Alliston, Ontario, Canada

Claim to Fame:

- Set a Guinness World Record in the 2018 Spartan Death Race held in Pittsfield, Vermont
- Crawled through mud and rocks for more than 26 miles (42 km) under barbed wire

Racers are determined. They won't give up.

determined: to have a strong wish to finish or achieve something

They learn about the race. Then they train for its course and challenges.

course: the path a race takes

UP NEXT!

The most extreme competitions in the world.

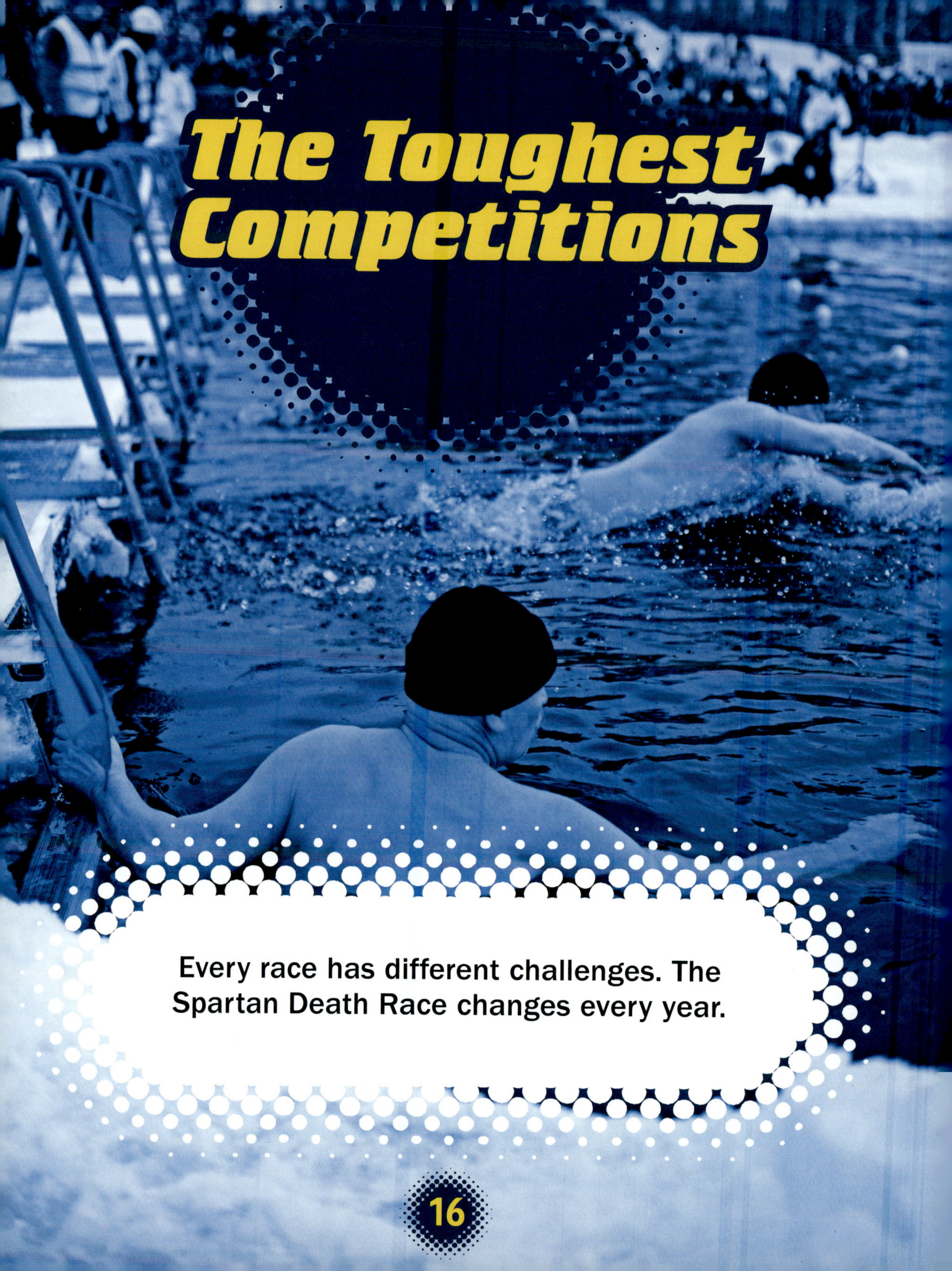

The Toughest Competitions

Every race has different challenges. The Spartan Death Race changes every year.

Racers swim in ice-cold water. They hike up mountains. They do burpees and even chop wood.

burpee: an exercise that includes a squat, a push-up, and jumping

The Marathon des Sables is in the Sahara Desert. Racers bring their own food. They run for six days.

The race is equal to about six marathons. Racers run 156 miles (250 km).

marathon: a running race that lasts 26.2 miles (42.2 km)

The Full Brutal is an extreme triathlon. Racers run, bike, and swim for 143.5 miles (230.9 km). The Double Brutal is twice as long!

triathlon: a race that has three different events

Endurance races are for tough athletes.
Only the toughest can endure to the finish line.

Glossary

burpee: an exercise that includes a squat, a push-up, and jumping

course: the path a race takes

cross-train: to do two or more workouts that train the whole body

determined: to have a strong wish to finish or achieve something

endurance: the ability to stay strong over a long period of time

marathon: a running race that lasts 26.2 miles (42.2 km)

triathlon: a race that has three different events

Check It Out!

Extreme Sports
https://www.ducksters.com/sports/extreme.php

Extreme Sports Facts
http://www.sciencekids.co.nz/sciencefacts/sports
/extremesports.html

Five Ways to Avoid Sports Injuries
https://kidshealth.org/en/kids/sport-safety.html?WT
.ac=ctg#catfit

Nagle, Jeanne. *Extreme Biking*. New York: Rosen, 2016.

Payment, Simone. *Extreme Rock Climbing*. New York: Rosen, 2020.

Waxman, Laura Hamilton. *Ninja Competitions*. Minneapolis: Lerner Publications, 2020.

Index

Photo Acknowledgments

Image credits: m-imagephotography/iStockphoto/Getty Images, p. 1; Milan M/Shutterstock.com, p. 1 (design elements); VectoRay/Shutterstock.com, p. 1 (design elements); JONATHAN NACKSTRAND/AFP/Getty Images, p. 4; U.S. Army Photo by Photographer (Sgt. Darron Salzer), p. 5; Dudarev Mikhail/Shutterstock.com, p. 6; Mladen Zivkovic/iStockphoto/Getty Images, p. 8; Flamingo Images/Shutterstock.com, p. 9; Stefan Holm/Shutterstock.com, p. 10; bbernard/Shutterstock.com, p. 11; Tom Gowanlock/Shutterstock.com, p. 12; Stefan Holm/Shutterstock.com, p. 13; Alfaguarilla/Shutterstock.com, p. 14; David Pereiras/Shutterstock.com, p. 15; VW PICS/Universal Images Group/Getty Images, p. 16; ActiveSteve/flickr (CC BY-ND 2.0), p. 17; JEAN-PHILIPPE KSIAZEK/AFP/Getty Images, p. 18; Martin BUREAU/AFP/Getty Images, p. 19; Jonathan NACKSTRAND/AFP/Getty Images, pp. 20, 21.

Cover: m-imagephotography/iStockphoto/Getty Images; rogistok/Shutterstock.com.